CORE WRITING SKILLS

How to Plan, Revise, and Edit Your Text

Sara Howell

PowerKids press

New York

Published in 2014 by The Rosen Publishing Group, Inc.
29 East 21st Street, New York, NY 10010

First Edition

Editor: Amelie von Zumbusch
Book Design: Andrew Povolny
Photo Research: Katie Stryker

Photo Credits: Cover Alexander Trinitatov/Shutterstock.com; pp. 4–5 Matthew Ennis/Shutterstock.com; p. 6 prudkov/Shutterstock.com; p. 7 tusharkoley/Shutterstock.com; p. 8 Hill Street Studios/Blend Images/Getty Images; p. 9 Jose Antonio Perez/Shutterstock.com; p. 10 Monkey Business Images/Shutterstock.com; p. 12 andamanec/Shutterstock.com; p. 13 Pressmaster/Shutterstock.com; p. 14 PCHT/Shutterstock.com; p. 16 Rubberball/Mike Kemp/Getty Images; p. 18 Lisa F. Young/Shutterstock.com; p. 19 Carlos Osorio/Toronto Star/Getty Images; p. 21 MilousSK/Shutterstock.com; p. 22 Fuse/Getty Images.

Library of Congress Cataloging-in-Publication Data

Howell, Sara.
  How to plan, revise, and edit your text / By Sara Howell. — First Edition.
    pages cm. — (Core writing skills)
  Includes index.
  ISBN 978-1-4777-2910-6 (library) — ISBN 978-1-4777-2999-1 (pbk.) —
  ISBN 978-1-4777-3069-0 (6-pack)
  1. English language—Composition and exercises—Juvenile literature. 2. Report writing—Juvenile literature. 3. Word processing—Juvenile literature. 4. Language arts. I. Title.
  PE1408.H68527 2014
  372.62'3—dc23
                          2013023806

Manufactured in the United States of America

CPSIA Compliance Information: Batch #W14PK4: For Further Information contact Rosen Publishing, New York, New York at 1-800-237-9932

CONTENTS

MAKING PLANS AND MAKING CHANGES

Sitting down to write may seem simple. However, good writing takes work. Before you begin, it is important to plan what you will say and how you will say it. After you have written a piece, you will need to check it for spelling and **grammar** mistakes. This is called editing. You should also reread your work and look for anything you would like to revise, or change and improve.

Planning, editing, and revising your work takes time. However, these are important skills that will greatly improve your writing. Even famous authors take time to plan, revise, and edit their work!

Writing Tip

Knowing that you will edit and revise your piece later gives you the freedom to make mistakes now. Don't worry about being perfect. Just write!

Every book you read has been carefully planned, edited, and revised. Planning, editing, and revising will make your own writing better, too!

One of the first things to figure out is what kind of text you will be writing. Some pieces give information about a **topic**. These are called explanatory texts. An opinion piece tells readers how a writer feels about a topic and then uses facts to show why. A narrative piece tells a true or made-up story.

The **structure**, or frame, of an explanatory text or opinion piece tends to be different from the

A personal narrative tells a true story from the author's life. For example, it might explain how the author met his best friend.

structure of a narrative. Even the kind of words you use might be different. Explanatory texts often use **formal** language. Narratives most often use informal language.

Writing Tip

The person who tells the story in a narrative is the narrator. The narrators of stories written in the first person speak of themselves as "I."

A report on Mount St. Helens, the volcano in Washington, would be an explanatory text.

You may be asked to write about topics that are unfamiliar, or new to you. To find out more about a topic, you will need to do some **research**, or careful study. Books, newspaper articles, and other printed **sources** are great places to start your research. You can also find a lot of information on the Internet.

Libraries are great places to find books and other printed sources. Most libraries also have computers that you can use to do research online.

Taking notes during your research can be very helpful. As you read, write down key words and ideas. When it is time to write, look back over your notes and put the main ideas into your own words.

Writing Tip

Websites run by museums, zoos, and the US government are good places to find reliable information on the Internet. However, not all websites are trustworthy.

If you need to learn about space exploration, you could check out the website of NASA, the National Aeronautics and Space Administration.

BUILDING A STRUCTURE

An organized structure will help you convey ideas and information clearly. The first part of your piece is the **introduction**. It states the topic and tells readers what the text will be about. The next part is called the body. It is the main part of the text. It usually has several **paragraphs**, or sections. The last part is the **conclusion**. This is where you can sum up ideas and give readers a sense of ending.

Making an outline will help you plan your piece's structure. Write down the parts of the piece. Then go over your notes and fill in information where it fits best.

It is easier to write your piece if you make an outline first. Using an outline also makes sure that your piece will be well organized.

I. Introduction to the Sun

II. Body

    A. Star

        1. Closest star

        2. Yellow dwarf star

        3. Sends out heat and light

    B. Size

        1. Biggest thing in solar system

        2. More than 100 times wider than Earth

    C. Orbiting

        1. "Orbit" means "to circle around"

        2. Earth's orbit = 1 year

III. Conclusion

GRAMMAR GUIDE

Editing is a big part of the writing process. When you edit, you fix mistakes. Be on the lookout for grammar mistakes. Grammar is the system of rules for how words combine to form sentences.

Writing Tip

Be sure your information is current, or up-to-date. Credible sources usually keep their information current, while other sites may not.

You should write, "Snow leopards are from Asia," but not "Snow leopards is pretty." The noun "snow leopards" and the verb "are" are both plural, but "is" is a singular verb.

Always check that you are using parts of speech correctly in a sentence. A noun is a person, place, or thing. Always use plural verbs, or action words, with plural nouns. Use adjectives, such as "soft," to describe nouns and adverbs, such as "softly," to describe verbs. Make sure to use only one **tense** throughout your piece. Don't slip back and forth between the present and the past!

People often use a red pen or pencil to mark their edits on pieces of writing. A bright color makes edits stand out on the paper.

PUNCTUATION AND SPELLING CHECKS

Another part of editing is checking **punctuation** and spelling. Be sure that the first word of each sentence starts with a capital letter. The names of people and places should be capitalized, too. All sentences should end with a period, exclamation point, or question mark. You should also check that you have used commas, apostrophes, and other punctuation marks correctly. If you are unsure, ask a parent or friend for help.

This bird is feeding its babies. When it means "belonging to it," "its" has no apostrophe. When it is short for "it is," though, "it's" does have an apostrophe.

Add apostrophe

V

"I ll meet you there!"
said Ana.
    Max watched her
dissappear over the hill.
He headed down the other
path. A small, noisy streem
                        a
ran alongside it.

Writing Tip

Quotes and lines of
dialogue should be put
inside double quotation
marks. Be sure to tell
readers who said the
words, too!

    As you read your
piece, keep an eye
out for words that are
misspelled, too. If you
do not know how to
spell a word, look it up
in a dictionary.

GO WITH THE FLOW

You'll also want to revise your piece. Read over what you have written and look for things that could be improved. As you reread, see if the piece flows well, or clearly moves from one idea to the next. Ask yourself if there are any parts that do not make sense.

Authors don't want to confuse readers! Make sure that your piece makes sense and is not missing any key information.

Add: The Sahara is a huge desert.
∨ It is in northern Africa.
The highest peak is Emi
↗ Koussi. This is in the Tibesti
Mountains. (It has several
Move (mountain ranges.)

Writing Tip

If you have used words that may be unfamiliar to readers, add definitions of those words to the text.

If you are writing an opinion piece, have you clearly shown why you feel a certain way?
Be sure your supporting facts back up your opinion. If you are writing an explanatory piece, ask yourself if you have conveyed your ideas and information clearly.

GIVING FEEDBACK

Sometimes you will be asked to read and comment on a classmate's work. The suggestions that you give someone on how to edit and revise a piece are called **feedback**. Good feedback will help your classmate improve his writing.

When giving feedback, make sure to mention not just ways to improve the piece, but also things that you think the author did well.

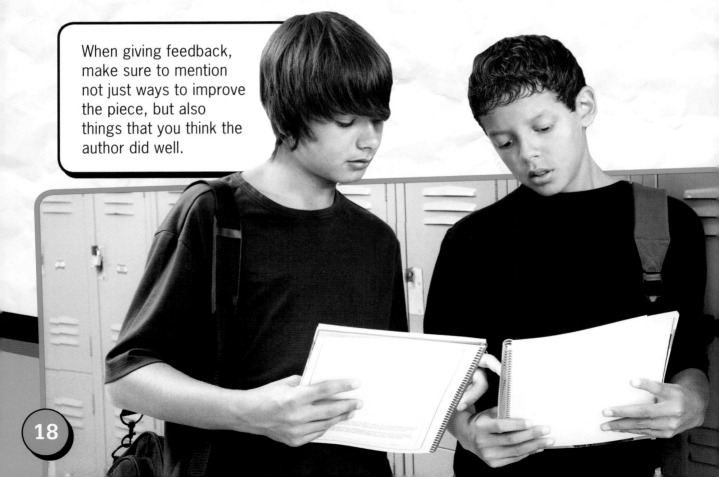

Sometimes teachers break classes up into writing groups. Each person in the group reads the other members' pieces and offers feedback on them.

Writing Tip

Even if you think someone's writing is good the way it is, try to think of at least one way in which it could be improved.

In your feedback, try to avoid saying that something is just good or bad. That does not give the writer much of an idea of how to improve. Instead, explain why you liked or disliked something. The more **specific**, or exact, you are with your feedback, the easier it will be for the writer to understand and use it.

TAKE YOUR TIME

A version of a piece of writing is called a **draft**. Each new draft includes edits and revisions that make the piece better. Start writing early enough so that you can set your piece aside for a few days. Then take it out and read it again as if you had never seen it before. If it were someone else's writing, what feedback would you give?

If other people have read your piece and given you feedback, you can use their ideas to revise as well. Do not be afraid to move large sections around or rewrite paragraphs that do not work.

Writing Tip

When you give yourself time to revise, you do not have to turn your paper in until you are happy with it!

The first version of your piece is also known as the first draft. The last version is often called the final draft. There can be several drafts in between.

USING TECHNOLOGY

Planning, editing, and revising are skills you can use for the rest of your life. Today's technology can make using these skills much easier. When you use a computer, you can add words, take out entire paragraphs, and cut and paste sections of your piece with just a few clicks.

You can even use your computer and the Internet to share your finished piece with others. Just imagine the feedback you might get from around the world!

Some computer programs automatically check for grammar and spelling mistakes. These give you a head start on editing your piece.

GLOSSARY

conclusion (kun-KLOO-zhun) The last part or ending of something.

draft (DRAFT) A version of a piece of writing.

feedback (FEED-bak) Suggestions from people who have reviewed something.

formal (FOR-mel) According to set rules.

grammar (GRA-mer) The rules of how words combine to form sentences.

introduction (in-truh-DUK-shun) A beginning part that explains what is going to follow.

paragraphs (PAR-uh-grafs) Groups of sentences about a certain subject or idea.

punctuation (punk-choo-WAY-shun) The use of periods, commas, and other marks to help make the meaning of a sentence clear.

research (rih-SERCH) Careful study.

sources (SORS-ez) Things that give facts or knowledge.

specific (spih-SIH-fik) Stated in a way that is clearly and easily understood.

structure (STRUK-cher) Form.

tense (TENS) The form of a verb that tells you when the action happened.

topic (TAH-pik) The subject of a piece of writing.

INDEX

WEBSITES

Due to the changing nature of Internet links, PowerKids Press has developed an online list of websites related to the subject of this book. This site is updated regularly. Please use this link to access the list: www.powerkidslinks.com/cws/revise/